Wilbur-Roo the Emu

ALEXANDRA STAUDT

ILLUSTRATIONS INSPIRED BY:
STORMI BINGHAM

ISBN 979-8-89130-341-6 (paperback)
ISBN 979-8-89130-342-3 (hardcover)
ISBN 979-8-89130-343-0 (digital)

Christian Faith Publishing
832 Park Avenue
Meadville, PA 16335
www.christianfaithpublishing.com

Printed in the United States of America

To G, thanks for always believing.

On a warm summer day
In a land far away

Lived Mama Emu
Who just laid something new

2

Through the shell of the egg beat a tiny new heart
A baby she knew she would love from the start

All babies are a gift from God above
And this one was sent for Mama Emu to love

With a crack in the shell
and a push of his feet
Out popped a baby for
his mother to meet!

His feathers were blue, and his eyes big and round
He smiled at his mama with his shell on the ground

Now what would she name him, she thought
For a baby so sweet and so new

"I've got it," she said, "I'll name him Wilbur-Roo"

Mama hugged his neck and
kissed his beak then said,

"Happy birthday, Wilbur-Roo. I love you!"

About the Author

Alexandra Staudt is a small-town Alabama writer who has enjoyed putting pen to paper since she was a little girl. Alex is an avid nonfiction writer. Married to her high school sweetheart, Alex is a veteran of the United States Air Force as well as a registered nurse. Inspired by the birth of her first child, she began writing books geared toward children, and *Wilbur-Roo the Emu* came to life. This is the first book in a series of books about a sweet, blue emu. In her free time, Alex enjoys reading, writing, traveling, and spending time with her family.

Printed in the USA
CPSIA information can be obtained
at www.ICGtesting.com
LVHW070609200924
791522LV00011B/171